THE QUESTION OF OUR SPEECH

THE LESSON OF BALZAC

THE QUESTION OF OUR SPEECH
THE LESSON OF BALZAC

Two Lectures

BY HENRY JAMES

BOSTON AND NEW YORK
HOUGHTON, MIFFLIN AND COMPANY
The Riverside Press, Cambridge
1905

COPYRIGHT 1905 BY HENRY JAMES
ALL RIGHTS RESERVED

Published October 1905

I
THE QUESTION OF OUR SPEECH

THE QUESTION OF OUR SPEECH [1]

I AM offered the opportunity of addressing you a few observations on a subject that should content itself, to my thinking, with no secondary place among those justly commended to your attention on such a day as this, and that yet will not, I dare say, have been treated before you, very often, as a matter especially inviting that attention. You will have been appealed to, at this season, and in preparation for this occasion, with admirable persuasion and admirable effect, I make no doubt, on behalf of many of the interests and ideals, scholarly, moral, social, you have here so happily pursued, many of the duties, responsibilities, opportunities

[1] Address to the graduating class at Bryn Mawr College, Pennsylvania, June 8, 1905; here printed with the restoration of a few passages omitted on that occasion.

you have learned, in these beautiful conditions, at the threshold of life, to see open out before you. These admonitions, taken together, will have borne, essentially, upon the question of culture, as you are expected to consider and cherish it; and some of them, naturally, will have pressed on the higher, the advanced developments of that question, those that are forever flowering above our heads and waving and rustling their branches in the blue vast of human thought. Others, meanwhile, will have lingered over the fundamentals, as we may call them, the solid, settled, seated elements of education, the things of which it is held, in general, that our need of being reminded of them must rarely be allowed to become a desperate or a feverish need. These underlying things, truths of tradition, of aspiration, of discipline, of training consecrated by experience, are understood as present in any liberal course of study or scheme of character; yet they permit of a certain renewed reference and slightly ceremonial insistence, perhaps, on high days and holidays; without the fear, on the part of any one concerned, of their falling too much into the category of the commonplace. I repeat, however, that there is a prime part of education, an element of the basis itself, in regard to which I shall probably remain within the bounds of safety in declaring that no explicit, no separate, no adequate plea will be likely to have ranged itself under any one of your customary heads of commemoration. If there are proprieties and values, perfect possessions of the educated spirit, clear humanities, as the old collegiate usage beautifully named them, that may be taken absolutely for granted, taken for granted as rendering any process of training simply possible, the indispensable preliminary I allude to, and that I am about to name, would easily indeed present itself in that light; thus confessing to its established character and its tacit intervention. A virtual consensus of the educated, of any gathered group, in regard to the *speech* that, among the idioms and articulations of the globe, they profess to make use of, may well strike us, in a given case, as a natural, an inevitable assumption. Without that consensus, to every appearance, the educative process cannot be thought of as at all even beginning; we readily perceive that without it the mere imparting of a coherent culture would never get under way. This imparting of a coherent culture is a matter of communication and response — each of which branches of an understanding involves the possession of a common language, with its modes of employment, its usage, its authority, its beauty, in working form; a medium of expression, in short, organized and developed. So obvious is such a truth that even at these periods of an especially excited consciousness of your happy ap-

OUR SPEECH

proximation to the ideal, your conquest, so far as it has proceeded, of the humanities aforesaid, of the great attainable amenities, you would not think of expecting that your not having failed to master the system of mere vocal sounds that renders your fruitful association with each other a thinkable thing should be made a topic of inquiry or of congratulation. You would say if you thought about the point at all: "Why, of course we speak in happy forms; we arrive here, arrive from our convenient homes, our wonderful schools, our growing cities, our great and glorious States, speaking in those happy forms in which people speak whose speech promotes the refinements (in a word the success) of intercourse, intellectual and social — not in any manner in which people speak whose speech frustrates, or hampers, or mocks at them. That conquest is behind us, and we invite no discussion of the question of whether we are articulate, whether we are intelligibly, or completely, expressive — we expose ourselves to none; the question of whether we are heirs and mistresses of the art of making ourselves satisfactorily heard, conveniently listened to, comfortably and agreeably understood."

Such, I say, is the assumption that everything must always have ministered to your making: so much as to stamp almost with a certain indecorum, on the face of the affair, any breach of the silence surrounding these familiar securities and serenities. I can only stand before you, accordingly, as a breaker of the silence; breaking it as gently, of course, as all the pleasant proprieties of this hour demand, but making the point that there is an element of fallacy — in plain terms a measurable mistake — in the fine confidence I am thus feeling my way to impute to you. It is needless to make sure of the basis of the process of communication and intercourse when it is clear, when it is positive, that such a basis exists and flourishes; but that is a question as to which the slightest shade of doubt is disquieting, disconcerting—fatal indeed; so that an exceptional inquiry into the case is then prescribed. I shall suggest our making this inquiry altogether — after having taken it thus as exceptionally demanded; making it rapidly, in the very limited way for which our present conditions allow us moments; but at least with the feeling that we are breaking ground where it had not hitherto, among us, strangely enough, been much broken, and where some measurable good may spring, for us, from our action.

If we may not then be said to be able to converse before we are able to talk (and study is essentially, above all in such a place as this, your opportunity to converse with your teachers and inspirers), so we may be said not to be able to "talk" before we are able to speak: whereby you easily see what we thus get. We may not be said to be able to study — and *a fortiori* do any of the things we study *for* — unless we are able to speak. All life therefore comes back to the question of our speech, the medium through which we communicate with each other; for all life comes back to the question of our relations with each other. These relations are made possible, are registered, are verily constituted, by our speech, and are successful (to repeat my word) in proportion as our speech is worthy of its great human and social function; is developed, delicate, flexible, rich — an adequate accomplished fact. The more it suggests and expresses the more we live by it — the more it promotes and enhances life. Its quality, its authenticity, its security, are hence supremely important for the general multifold opportunity, for the dignity and integrity, of our existence.

OUR SPEECH

These truths, you see, are incontestable; yet though you are daughters, fortunate in many respects, of great commonwealths that have been able to render you many attentions, to surround you with most of the advantages of peace and plenty, it is none the less definite that there will have been felt to reign among you, in general, no positive mark whatever, public or private, of an effective consciousness of any of them; the consciousness, namely — a sign of societies truly possessed of light — that no civilized body of men and women has ever left so vital an interest to run wild, to shift, as we say, all for itself, to stumble and flounder, through mere adventure and accident, in the common dust of life, to pick up a living, in fine, by the wayside and the ditch. Of the degree in which a society is civilized the vocal form, the vocal tone, the personal, social accent and sound of its intercourse, have always been held to give a direct reflection. That sound, that vocal form, the touchstone of manners, is the note, the representative note—representative of its having (in our poor, imperfect human degree) achieved civilization. Judged in this light, it must frankly be said, our civilization remains strikingly *un*achieved: the last of American idiosyncrasies, the last by which we can be conceived as " represented " in the international concert of culture, would be the pretension to a tone-standard, to our wooing comparison with that of other nations. The French, the Germans, the Italians, the English perhaps in particular, and many other people, Occidental and Oriental, I surmise, not excluding the Turks and the Chinese, have for the symbol of education, of civility, a tone-standard; we alone flourish in undisturbed and — as in the sense of so many other of our connections — in something like sublime unconsciousness of any such possibility.

OUR SPEECH

It is impossible, in very fact, to have a tone-standard without the definite preliminary of a *care* for tone, and against a care for tone, it would very much appear, the elements of life in this country, as at present conditioned, violently and increasingly militate. At one or two reasons for this strange but consummate conspiracy I shall in a moment ask you to glance with me, but in the meanwhile I should go any length in agreeing with you about any such perversity, on the part of parents and guardians, pastors and masters, as their expecting the generations, whether of young women or young men, to arrive at a position of such comparative superiority alone — unsupported and unguided. There is no warrant for the placing on these inevitably rather light heads and hearts, on any company of you, assaulted, in our vast vague order, by many pressing wonderments, the *whole* of the burden of a care for tone. A care for tone is part of a care for many other things besides; for the fact, for the value, of good breeding, above all, as to which tone unites with various other personal, social signs to bear testimony. The idea of good breeding — without which intercourse fails to flower into fineness, without which human relations bear but crude and tasteless fruit — is one of the most precious conquests of civilization, the very core of our social heritage; but in the transmission of which it becomes us much more to be active and interested than merely passive and irresponsible participants. It is an idea, the idea of good breeding (in other words, simply the idea of *secure* good manners), for which, always, in every generation, there is yet more, and yet more, to be done; and no danger would be more lamentable than that of the real extinction, in our hands, of so sacred a flame. Flames, however, even the most sacred, do not go on burning of themselves; they require to be kept up; handed on the torch needs to be from one group of patient and competent watchers to another. The possibility, the preferability, of people's speaking as people speak when their speech has had for them a signal importance, is a matter to be kept sharply present; from that comes support, comes example, comes authority — from that comes the inspiration of those comparative beginners of life, the hurrying children of time, who are but too exposed to be worked upon, by a hundred circumstances, in a different and inferior sense. You don't speak soundly and agreeably, you don't speak neatly and consistently, unless you *know* how you speak, how you may, how you should, how you shall speak, unless you have discriminated, unless you have noticed differences and suffered from violations and vulgarities; and you have not this positive consciousness, you are incapable of any reaction of taste or sensibility worth mentioning, unless a great deal of thought of the matter has been taken *for* you.

Taking thought, in this connection, is what I mean by obtaining a tone-standard — a clear criterion of the best usage and example: which is but to recognize, once for all, that avoiding vulgarity, arriving at lucidity, pleasantness, charm, and contributing by the mode and the degree of utterance a colloquial, a genial value even to an inevitably limited quantity of intention, of thought, is an art to be acquired and cultivated, just as much as any of the other, subtler, arts of life. There are plenty of influences round about us that make for an imperfect disengagement of the human side of vocal sound, that make for the confused, the ugly, the flat, the thin, the mean, the helpless, that reduce articulation to an easy and ignoble minimum, and so keep it as little distinct as possible from the grunting, the squealing, the barking or the roaring of animals. I do not mean to say that civility of utterance may not become an all but unconscious beautiful habit — I mean to say, thank goodness, that this is exactly what it *may* become. But so to succeed it must be a collective and associated habit; for the greater the number of persons speaking well, in given conditions, the more that number will tend to increase, and the smaller the number the more that number will tend to shrink and lose itself in the desert of the common. Contact and communication, a beneficent contagion, bring about the happy state — the state of sensibility to tone, the state of recognizing, and responding to, certain vocal sounds *as* tone, and recognizing and reacting from certain others as negations of tone: negations the more offensive in proportion as they have most enjoyed impunity. You will have, indeed, in any at all aspiring cultivation of tone, a vast mass of assured impunity, of immunity on the wrong side of the line, to reckon with. There are in every quarter, in our social order, impunities of aggression and corruption in plenty; but there are none, I think, showing so unperturbed a face — wearing, I should slangily say, if slang were permitted me here, so impudent a "mug" — as the forces assembled to make you believe that no form of speech is provably better than another, and that just this matter of "care" is an affront to the majesty of sovereign ignorance. Oh, I don't mean to say that you will find in the least a clear field and nothing but favor! The difficulty of your case is exactly the ground of my venturing thus to appeal to you. That there is difficulty, that there is a great blatant, blowing dragon to slay, can only constitute, as it appears to me, a call of honor for generous young minds, something of a trumpet-sound for tempers of high courage.

And now, of course, there are questions

you may ask me: as to what I more intimately mean by speaking "well," by speaking "ill;" as to what I more definitely mean by "tone" and by the "negation" of tone; as to where you are to recognize the presence of the exemplary rightness I have referred you to — as to where you are to see any standard raised to the breeze; and above all, as to my reasons for referring with such emphasis to the character of the enemy you are to overcome. I am able, I think, to satisfy you all the way; but even in so doing I shall still feel our question to be interesting, as a whole, out of proportion to any fractions of an hour we may now clutch at; feel that if I could only treat it with a freer hand and more margin I might really create in you a zeal to follow it up. I mean, then, by speaking well, in the first place, speaking under the influence of *observation* — your own. I mean speaking with consideration for the forms and shades of our language, a consideration so inbred that it has become instinctive and well-nigh unconscious and automatic, as all the habitual, all the inveterate amenities of life become. By the forms and shades of our language I mean the innumerable differentiated, discriminated units of sound and sense that lend themselves to audible production, to enunciation, to intonation: those innumerable units that have, each, an identity, a quality, an outline, a shape, a clearness, a fineness, a sweetness, a richness, that have, in a word, a value, which it is open to us, as lovers of our admirable English tradition, or as cynical traitors to it, to preserve or to destroy.

Many of these units are, for instance, our syllables, emphasized or unemphasized, our parts of words, or often the whole word itself, our parts of sentences, coming in *for* value and subject to be marked or missed, honored or dishonored — to use the term we use for checks at banks — as a note of

OUR SPEECH

sound. Many of them are in particular our simple vowel-notes and our consonantal, varying, shifting — shifting in relation and connection, as to value and responsibility and place — and capable of a complete effect, or of a complete absence of effect, according as a fine ear and a fine tongue, or as a coarse ear and a coarse tongue, preside at the use of them. All our employment of constituted sounds, syllables, sentences, comes back to the way we say a thing, and it is very largely by saying, all the while, that we live and play our parts. I am asking you to take it from me, as the very moral of these remarks, that the way we say a thing, or fail to say it, fail to learn to say it, has an importance in life that it is impossible to overstate — a far-reaching importance, as the very hinge of the relation of man to man. I am asking you to take that truth well home and hold it close to your hearts, setting your backs to the wall to defend it, heroically, when need may be. For need will be, among us, as I have already intimated, and as I shall proceed in a moment, though very briefly, to show you further: you must be prepared for much vociferous demonstration of the plea that the way we say things — the way we "say" in general — has as little importance as possible. Let the demonstration proceed, let the demonstration abound, let it be as vociferous as it will, if you only meanwhile hug the closer the faith I thus commend to you; for you will very presently perceive that the more this vain contention does make itself heard, the more it insists, the sooner it shall begin to flounder waist-high in desert sands. Nothing, sayable or said, that pretends to expression, to value, to consistency, in whatever interest, but finds itself practically confronted, at once, with the tone-question: the only refuge from which is the mere making of a noise — since simple noise is the sort of sound in which tone ceases to exist. To simple toneless noise, as an argument for indifference to discriminated speech, you may certainly then listen as philosophically as your nerves shall allow.

But the term I here apply brings me meanwhile to my second answer to your three or four postulated challenges — the question of what I mean by speaking badly. I might reply to you, very synthetically, that I mean by speaking badly speaking as millions and millions of supposedly educated, supposedly civilized persons — that is the point — of both sexes, in our great country, habitually, persistently, imperturbably, and I think for the most part all unwittingly, speak: that form of satisfaction to you being good enough — isn't it? — to cover much of the ground. But I must give you a closer account of the evil against which I warn you, and I think none is so close as this: that speaking badly is speaking with that want of attention to speech that we should blush to see any other of our personal functions compromised by — any other controllable motion, or voluntary act, of our lives. Want of attention, in any act, results in a graceless and unlighted effect, an effect of accident and misadventure; and it strikes me in this connection that there is no better comprehensive description of our vocal habits as a nation, in their vast, monotonous flatness and crudity, than this aspect and air of unlightedness — which presents them as matters going on, gropingly, helplessly, empirically, almost dangerously (perilously, that is, to life and limb), in the dark. To walk in the dark, dress in the dark, eat in the dark, is to run the chance of breaking our legs, of misarranging our clothes, of besmearing our persons; and speech may figure for us either as the motion, the food, or the clothing of intercourse, as you will. To do things "unlightedly" is accordingly to do them without neatness or completeness — and to accept that doom is simply to accept the doom of the slovenly.

Our national use of vocal sound, in men and women alike, *is* slovenly — an absolutely inexpert daub of unapplied tone. It leaves us at the mercy of a medium that, as I say, is incomplete; which sufficiently accounts, as regards our whole vocal manifestation, for the effect of a want of finish. Noted sounds have their extent and their limits, their mass, however concentrated, and their edges; and what is the speech of a given society but a series, a more or less rich complexity, of noted sounds? Nothing is commoner than to see throughout our country, young persons of either sex—for the phenomenon is most marked, I think, for reasons I will touch on, in the newer generations — whose utterance can only be indicated by pronouncing it destitute of any approach to an emission of the consonant. It becomes thus a mere helpless slobber of disconnected vowel noises

—the weakest and cheapest attempt at human expression that we shall easily encounter, I imagine, in any community pretending to the general instructed state. Observe, too, that the vowel sounds in themselves, at this rate, quite fail of any purity, for the reason that our consonants contribute to the drawing and modeling of our vowels — just as our vowels contribute to the coloring, to the painting, as we may call it, of our consonants, and that any frequent repetition of a vowel depending for all rounding and shaping on another vowel alone lays upon us an effort of the thorax under which we inevitably break down. Hence the undefined noises that I refer to when consonantal sound drops out; drops as it drops, for example, among those vast populations to whose lips, to whose ear, it is so rarely given to form the terminal letter of our "Yes," or to hear it formed. The abject "Yeh-eh" (the ugliness of the drawl is not easy to represent) which usurps the

OUR SPEECH

place of that interesting vocable makes its nearest approach to deviating into the decency of a final consonant when it becomes a still more questionable " Yeh-ep."

Vast numbers of people, indeed, even among those who speak very badly, appear to grope instinctively for some restoration of the missing value even at the cost of inserting it between words that begin and end with vowels. You will perfectly hear persons supposedly " cultivated," the very instructors of youth sometimes themselves, talk of vanilla-r-ice-cream, of California-r-oranges, of Cuba-r-and Porto Rico, of Atalanta-r- in Calydon, and (very resentfully) of " the idea-r-of" any intimation that their performance and example in these respects may not be immaculate. You will perfectly hear the sons and daughters of the most respectable families disfigure in this interest, and for this purpose, the pleasant old names of Papa and Mamma. " Is Popper-up stairs ? " and "is Mommer-in the parlor?" pass for excellent household speech in millions of honest homes. If the English say throughout, and not only sometimes, Papa and Mama, and the French say Papa and Maman, they say them consistently — and Popper, with an "r," but illustrates our loss, much to be regretted, alas, of the power to emulate the clearness of the vowel-cutting, an art as delicate in its way as gem-cutting, in the French word. You will, again, perfectly hear a gentle hostess, solicitous for your comfort, tell you that if you wish to lie down there is a sofa-r-in your room. No one is "thought any the worse of" for saying these things; even though it be distinct that there are circles, in other communities, the societies still keeping the touchstone of manners, as I have called our question, in its place, where they would be punctually noted. It is not always a question of an *r*, however — though the letter, I grant, gets terribly little rest among those great masses of our population who strike us, in the boundless West perhaps especially, as, under some strange impulse received toward consonantal recovery of balance, making it present even in words from which it is absent, bringing it in everywhere as with the small vulgar effect of a sort of morose grinding of the back teeth. There are, you see, sounds of a mysterious intrinsic meanness, and there are sounds of a mysterious intrinsic frankness and sweetness; and I think the recurrent note I have indicated — fatherr and motherr and otherr, waterr and matterr and scatterr, harrd and barrd, parrt, starrt, and (dreadful to say) arrt (the repetition it is that drives home the ugliness), are signal specimens of what becomes of a custom of utterance out of which the principle of taste has dropped.

If I speak, as to these matters of tone, I may add, of intrinsic meanness and intrinsic sweetness, there is also no doubt that association, cumulation, the context of a given sound and the company we perceive it to be keeping, are things that have much to say to our better or worse impression. What has become of the principle of taste, at all events, when the *s*, too, breaks in, or breaks out, all unchecked and unchided, in such forms of impunity as Some-wheres-else and Nowheres-else, as A good ways-on and A good ways-off? — vulgarisms with which a great deal of general credit for what we good-naturedly call "refinement" appears so able to coexist. Credit for what we good-naturedly call refinement — since our national, our social good nature is, experimentally, inordinate — appears able to coexist with a thousand other platitudes and poverties of tone, aberrations too numerous for me to linger on in these very limited moments, but in relation to which all the flatly-drawling group — gawd and dawg, sawft and lawft, gawne and lawst and frawst — may stand as a hint.

Let me linger only long enough to add a mention of the deplorable effect of the almost total loss, among innumerable speakers, of any approach to purity in the sound of the *e*. It is converted, under this particularly ugly blight, into a *u* which is itself unaccompanied with any dignity of intention, which makes for mere ignoble thickness and turbidity. For choice, perhaps, "vurry," "Amurrica," "Philadulphia," "tullegram," "twuddy" (what becomes of "twenty" here is an ineptitude truly beyond any alliteration), and the like, descend deepest into the abyss. It is enough to say of those things that they substitute limp, slack, passive tone for clear, clean, active, tidy tone, and that they are typical, thereby, of an immense body of limpness and slackness and cheapness. This note of cheapness — of the cheap and easy — is especially fatal to any effect of security of intention in the speech of a society, for it is scarce necessary to remind you that there are two very different kinds of ease: the ease that comes from the facing, the conquest of a difficulty, and the ease that comes from the vague dodging of it. In the one case you gain facility, in the other case you get mere looseness. In the one case the maintenance of civility of speech costs what it must — which is a price we should surely blush to hear spoken of as too great for our inaptitude and our indolence, our stupidity and our frivolity, to pay.

I must invite you indeed to recognize with me, at whatever cost to any possible share in our national self-complacency, that we encounter in all this connection a certain portent in our sky, a certain lion in our path, complications duly to be reckoned with; encounter them in the circumstance of the *voice* of our people at large, our people abundantly schooled and newspapered, abundantly housed, fed, clothed, salaried and taxed — which happens to fall on no expert attention you may easily note, as the finest or fullest or richest of the voices of the nations: this, moreover, least of all among our women, younger and older, as to whom in general, and as to the impression made by whom, the question of voice ever most comes up and has most importance. The *vox Americana* then, frankly, is for the spectator, or perhaps I should say for the auditor of life, as he travels far and wide, one of the stumbling-blocks of our continent — having no claim to be left out of account in any discussion of the matter before us. It remains for the moment, this collective vocal presence, this preponderant vocal sign, what a convergence of inscrutable forces (climatic, social, political, theological, moral, " psychic ") has made it and failed to make it: so that I shall ask you to let it stand for you thus as a *temporarily-final* fact — so stand long enough to allow me to say that, whatever else it is, it has been, among the organs of the schooled and newspapered races, perceptibly the most abandoned to its fate. That truth about it is more to our purpose than any other, and throws much light, I am convinced, on the manner in which it affects and afflicts us. I shall go so far as to say that there is no such thing as a voice pure and simple: there is only, for any business of appreciation, the voice *plus* the way it is employed; an employment determined here by a greater number of influences than we can now go into—beyond affirming at least, that when such influences, in general, have acted for a long time we think of them as having made not only the history of the voice, but positively the history of the national character, almost the history of the people.

It would take thus too long to tell you why the English voice, or why the French, or why the Italian, is so free to strike us as *not* neglected, not abandoned to its fate; as having much rather been played upon, through the generations, by a multitude of causes which have finally begotten, in each of these instances, as means to an end, a settled character, a certain ripeness, finality and felicity. I cannot but regard the unsettled character and the inferior quality of the colloquial *vox Americana* — and I speak here but of the poor dear distracted organ itself — as in part a product of that mere state of indifference to a speech-standard and to a tone-standard on which I have been insisting. The voice, I repeat, is, as to much of its action and much of its effect, not a separate, lonely, lost thing, but largely what the tone, the conscious, intended, associated tone, makes of it — and what the tone that has none of these attributes falls short of making; so that if we here again, as a people, take care, if we take even common care, of the question, for fifty years or thereabout, I have no doubt we shall in due course find the subject of our solicitude put on, positively, a surface, find it reflect and repay the enlightened effort. We shall find that, while we have been so well occupied, the vocal, the tonic possibilities within us all, grateful to us for the sense of a flattering interest, of the offer of a new life, have been taking care, better care, excellent care, of *themselves*. The experiment, absolutely, would be worth trying — and perhaps not on so formidable a scale of time either. We see afresh, at any rate, into what interesting relations and ramifications our topic opens out — if only as an illustration of what we may do for ourselves by merely *raising* our question and setting it up before us. With it verily we raise and set up the question of our manners as well, for that is indissolubly involved. To discriminate, to learn to find our way among noted sounds, find it as through the acquisition of a new ear; to begin to prefer form to the absence of form, to distinguish color from the absence of color — all this amounts to substituting manner for the absence of manner: whereby it is *manners themselves*, or something like a sketchy approach to a dim gregarious conception of them, that we shall (delicious thought!) begin to work round to the notion of.

I should also not fail to remind you, for keeping all things clear, that I refer here not specifically, in fact not directly at all, to our handling of the English language as such — even though wonderful enough the adventure may be to which, in our so unceremonious, so simplified and simplifying conditions, we are treating that ancient and battered but still nobly robust and at the same time tenderly vulnerable idiom. I am not doing so, because this matter of the use and abuse of our mother-tongue would be another theme altogether, in spite of its close alliance with the question before us. Yet I cannot wholly forget that the adventure, as I name it, of our idiom and the adventure of our utterance have been fundamentally the same adventure and the same experience; that they at a given period migrated together, immigrated together, into the great raw world in which they were to be cold-shouldered and neglected together, left to run wild and lose their way together. They have suffered and strayed together, and the future of the one, we must after all remember, is necessarily and logically the prospect or the doom of the other. Keep in sight the so interesting historical truth that no language, so far back as our acquaintance with history goes, has known any such ordeal, any such stress and strain, as was to await the English in this huge new community it was so unsuspectingly to help, at first, to father and mother. It came *over*, as the phrase is, came over originally without fear and without guile — but to find itself transplanted to spaces it had never dreamed, in its comparative humility, of covering, to conditions it had never dreamed, in its comparative innocence, of meeting; to find itself grafted, in short, on a social and political order that was both without previous precedent and example and incalculably expansive.

Taken on the whole by surprise it may doubtless be said to have behaved as well as unfriended heroine ever behaved in dire predicament — refusing, that is, to be frightened quite to death, looking about for a *modus vivendi*, consenting to live, preparing to wait on developments. I say " unfriended " heroine because that is exactly my point: that whereas the great idioms of Europe in general have grown up at home and in the family, the ancestral circle (with their migrations all comfortably prehistoric), our transported maiden, our unrescued Andromeda, our medium of utterance, was to be disjoined from all the associations, the other presences, that had attended her, that had watched for her and with her, that had helped to form her manners and her voice, her taste and her genius.

THE QUESTION OF

It is the high modernism of the conditions now surrounding, on this continent, the practice of our language that makes of this chapter in its history a new thing under the sun; and I use that term as the best for expressing briefly ever so many striking actualities. If you reflect a moment you will see how unprecedented is in fact this uncontrolled assault of most of our circumstances — and in the forefront of them the common school and the newspaper — upon what we may call our linguistic *position*. Every language has its position, which, with its particular character and genius, is its most precious property — the element in it we are most moved (if we have any feeling in the connection at all) to respect, to confirm, to consecrate. What we least desire to do with these things is to give them, in our happy phrase, "away;" and we must allow that if this be none the less what has really happened in our case the reason for the disaster resides in the seemingly overwhelming (for the time at least) forces of betrayal. To the American common school, to the American newspaper, and to the American Dutchman and Dago, as the voice of the people describes them, we have simply handed over our property — not exactly bound hand and foot, I admit, like Andromeda awaiting her Perseus, but at least distracted, dishevelled, despoiled, divested of that beautiful and becoming drapery of native atmosphere and circumstance which had, from far back, made, on its behalf, for practical protection, for a due tenderness of interest.

I am perfectly aware that the common school and the newspaper are influences that shall often have been named to you, exactly, as favorable, as positively and actively contributive, to the prosperity of our idiom ; the answer to which is that the matter depends, distinctly, on what is meant by prosperity. It is prosperity, of a sort, that a hundred million people, a few years hence, will be unanimously, loudly—above all loudly, I think!— speaking it, and that, moreover, many of these millions will have been artfully wooed and weaned from the Dutch, from the Spanish, from the German, from the Italian, from the Norse, from the Finnish, from the Yiddish even, strange to say, and (stranger still to say) even from the English, for the sweet sake, or the sublime consciousness, as we may perhaps put it, of speaking, of talking, for the first time in their lives, *really* at their ease. There are many things our now so profusely imported and, as is claimed, quickly assimilated foreign brothers and sisters may do at their ease in this country, and at two minutes' notice, and without asking any one else's leave or taking any circumstance whatever into account — any save an infinite uplifting sense of freedom and facility; but the thing they may best do is play, to their heart's content, with the English language, or, in other words, dump their mountain of promiscuous material into the foundations of the American. As to any claim made for the newspapers, there would be far more to say than I can thus even remotely allude to ; it will suffice, however, if I just recall to you that contribution to the idea of expression which you must feel yourselves everywhere getting, wherever you turn, from the mere noisy vision of their ubiquitous page, bristling with rude effigies and images, with vociferous " headings," with letterings, with black eruptions of print, that we seem to measure by feet rather than by inches, and that affect us positively as the roar of some myriad-faced monster — as the grimaces, the shouts, shrieks and yells, ranging over the whole gamut of ugliness, irrelevance, dissonance, of a mighty maniac who has broken loose and who is running amuck through the spheres alike of sense and of sound. So it is, surely, that our wonderful daily press *most* vividly reads us the lesson of *values*, of just proportion and just appreciation, lights the air for this question of our improvement.

The truth is that, excellent for diffusion, for vulgarization, for simplification, the common schools and the " daily paper " define themselves before us as quite below the mark for discrimination and selection, for those finer offices of vigilance and criticism in the absence of which the forms of civility, with the forms of speech most setting the example, drift out to sea. Our case is accordingly not that we should indulge in jealousy, in care, less than other communities, but that we are the community in the world who should precisely most indulge in them. We should rather sit up at night with our preoccupation than close our eyes by day as well as by night. All the while we sleep the vast contingent of aliens whom we make welcome, and whose main contention, as I say, is that,

OUR SPEECH

from the moment of their arrival, they have just as much property in our speech as we have, and just as good a right to do what they choose with it — the grand right of the American being to do just what he chooses " over here " with anything and everything: all the while we sleep the innumerable aliens are sitting up (*they* don't sleep!) to work their will on their new inheritance and prove to us that they are without any finer feeling or more conservative instinct of consideration for it, more fond, unutterable association with it, more hovering, caressing curiosity about it, than they may have on the subject of so many yards of freely figured oilcloth, from the shop, that they are preparing to lay down, for convenience, on kitchen floor or kitchen staircase. Oilcloth is highly convenient, and our loud collective medium of intercourse doubtless strikes these new householders as wonderfully resisting " wear " — with such wear as it gets! — strikes them as an excellent bargain: durable, tough, cheap.

Just here it is that I may be asked, meanwhile — or that you are likely to be asked in your turn, so far as you may be moved to make anything of these admonitions — whether a language be not always a living organism, fed by the very breath of those who employ it, whoever these may happen to be; of those who carry it with them, on their long road, as their specific experience grows larger and more complex, and who need it to help them to meet this expansion. The question is whether it be not either no language at all, or only a very poor one, if it have not in it to respond, from its core, to the constant appeal of time, perpetually demanding new tricks, new experiments, new amusements of it: so to respond without losing its characteristic balance. The answer to that is, a hundred times, "Yes," assuredly, so long as the conservative interest, which should always predominate, remains, equally, the constant quantity; remains an embodied, constituted, inexpugnable thing. The conservative interest is really as indispensable for the institution of speech as for the institution of matrimony. Abate a jot of the quantity, and, much more, of the quality, of the consecration required, and we practically find ourselves emulating the beasts, who prosper as well without a vocabulary as without a marriage-service. It is easier to overlook any question of speech than to trouble about it, but then it is also easier to snort or neigh, to growl or to " meaow," than to articulate and intonate.

With this hint, for you, of the manner in which the forces of looseness are in possession of the field, you may well wonder where you are to meet the influences of example and authority, as we can only call them, my failure to undertake to indicate some attesting presence of which would leave me in such sore straits. Well, I grant you here that I am at a loss to name you particular and unmistakable, edifying and illuminating groups or classes, from which this support is to be derived; since nothing, unfortunately, more stares us in the face than the frequent failure of such comfort in those quarters where we might, if many things were different, most look for it. When you have heard a fond parent remark, in jealous majesty, to a conscientious instructor of youth, that there is no call for "interference" with the vocal noises of a loved son or daughter whose vocal noises have been unmoderated and uncontrolled since the day of birth, and that these graces quite satisfy the sense of the home-circle; and when, to match such an attitude, you have heard an unawakened teacher disclaim responsibility for any such element as the tone-element and the voice-element in the forming of a young intelligence: when you

OUR SPEECH

have been present at such phenomena you will not unnaturally feel that the case is bewildering, feel yourselves perhaps even tragically committed to a doom. Cling, none the less, always, to a working faith, and content yourselves — if you can't encounter complete pleasantly-speaking companies, in any number — with encountering, blessedly, here and there, articulate individuals, torch-bearers, as we may rightly describe them, guardians of the sacred flame. It is not a question, however, so much of simply meeting them, as of attending to them, of making your profit of them, when you do meet. If they be at all adequate representatives of some decent tradition, you will find the interest of a new world, a whole extension of life, open to you in the attempt to estimate, in the habit of observing, in their speech, all that such a tradition consists of. Begin to exercise your attention on that, and let the consequences sink into your spirit. At first dimly, but then more and more distinctly, you will find yourselves noting, comparing, preferring, at last positively emulating and imitating.

Imitating, yes; I commend to you, earnestly and without reserve, as the first result and concomitant of observation, the imitation of formed and finished utterance wherever, among all the discords and deficiencies, that music steals upon your ear. The more you listen to it the more you will love it — the more you will wonder that you could ever have lived without it. What I thus urge upon you, you see, is a consciousness, an acute consciousness, absolutely; which is a proposition and a name likely enough to raise among many of your friends a protest. "Conscious, imitative speech — is n't that more dreadful than anything else?" It's not "dreadful," I reply, any more than it's ideal: the matter depends on the stage of development it represents. It's an awkwardness, in your situation, that your own stage is an early one, and that you have found, round about you — outside of these favoring shades — too little help. Therefore your consciousness will now represent the phase of awakening, and that will last what it must. Unconsciousness is beautiful when it means that our knowledge has passed into our conduct and our life; has become, as we say, a second nature. But the opposite state is the door through which it has to pass, and which is, inevitably, sometimes, rather straight and narrow. This squeeze is what we pay for having revelled too much in ignorance. Keep up your hearts, all the same, keep them up to the pitch of confidence in that " second nature " of which I speak; the perfect possession of this highest of the civilities, the sight, through the narrow portal, of the blue horizon across the valley, the wide fair country in which your effort will have settled to the most exquisite of instincts, in which you will taste all the savor of gathered fruit, and in which perhaps, at last, *then*, "in solemn troops and sweet societies," you may, sounding the clearer notes of intercourse as only women can, become yourselves models and missionaries, perhaps a little even martyrs, of the good cause.

II

THE LESSON OF BALZAC

THE LESSON OF BALZAC[1]

I HAVE found it necessary, at the eleventh hour, to sacrifice to the terrible question of time a very beautiful and majestic approach that I had prepared to the subject on which I have the honor of addressing you. I recognize it as impossible to ask you to linger with me on that pillared portico — paved with marble, I beg you to believe, and overtwined with charming flowers. I must invite you to pass straight into the house and bear with me there as if I had already succeeded in beginning to interest you. Let us assume, therefore, that we have exchanged some ideas on the question of the beneficent play of criticism, and that I have even ingeniously struck it off that <u>criticism is the</u>

---

[1] Delivered for the first time before the Contemporary Club of Philadelphia, January 12, 1905, and repeated on various occasions elsewhere. Several passages omitted in delivery — one of considerable length — have been restored.

only gate of appreciation, just as appreciation is, in regard to a work of art, the only gate of enjoyment. You may wonder perhaps why I speak as if we were possessed, in our conditions, of a literary court of appeal, and I hasten to say that the appeal I think of is precisely from the general judgment, and not to it; is to the particular judgment altogether: by which I mean to that quantity of opinion, very small at all times, but at all times infinitely precious, that is capable of giving some intelligible account of itself. Where, among us, at this time of day, this element of the lucid report of impressions received, of estimates formed, of intentions understood, of values attached, is exactly to be looked for — that is another branch of the question, to which I am afraid I should have to devote quite another discourse. I do not propose for a moment to invite you to blink the fact that our huge Anglo-Saxon array of producers and readers — and especially our vast cis-Atlantic multitude — presents production uncontrolled, production untouched by criticism, unguided, unlighted, uninstructed, unashamed, on a scale that is really a new thing in the world. It is all the complete reversal of any proportion, between the elements, that was ever seen before. It is the biggest flock straying without shepherds, making its music without a sight of the classic crook, beribboned or other, without a sound of the sheepdog's bark — wholesome note, once in a way — that has ever found room for pasture. The very opposite has happened from what might have been expected to happen. The shepherds have diminished as the flock has increased — quite as if number and quantity had got beyond them, or even as if their charge had turned, by some uncanny process, to a pack of ravening wolves. Let us none the less assume that we may still find two or three of the fraternity hiding under a hedge or astride of some upper limb of a tree; let us even assume that if we set rightly, if we set tactfully about it, we may establish again some friendly connection with them.

Putting, on this basis, then, all our heads together, we may become aware of an intelligent gratitude, deep within our breasts, to any author who consents to fit with a certain fulness of presence and squareness of solidity into one of the conscious categories of our attention. There are literary figures in plenty that scarce fill out even the smaller of these critical receptacles; there are others, on the contrary, that almost strain the larger to breaking. It is to these latter that interested contemplation most fondly attaches itself — to that degree, really, that there seems, on any good occasion, more and more about them to be said. They have the great sign that their immediate presence causes our ideas, whether about life in general or about the art they have exemplified in particular, to revive and breathe again, to multiply, more or less to swarm. I must profess that no Novelist—since we are by common consent confining our attention to that great Company — no Novelist, to my sense, so rewards consideration as he or she (and I emphasize the liberality of my " she ") who offers the critical spirit this opportunity for a certain intensity of educative practice. The lesson of Balzac, whom we thus march straight up to, is that he offers it as no other members of the company can pretend to do.

For there are members of the company who scarce produce the effect in question at all. Take, to begin with, close at Balzac's side, his illustrious contemporary Madame George Sand, so suggestive, so affirmative, so instructive, as a dealer with life, as an eloquent exponent of her own, as what we call to-day a Personality equipped and armed, but of an artistic complexion so comparatively smooth and simple, so happily harmonious, that her work, taken together, presents about as few pegs for analysis to hang upon as if it were a large, polished, gilded Easter egg, the pride of a sweet-shop if not the treasure of a museum. Let me add, further — so far as it is a question of the nameable sisterhood too — that Jane Austen, with all her light felicity, leaves us hardly more curious of her process, or of the experience in her that fed it, than the brown thrush who tells his story from the garden bough; and this, I freely confess, in spite of her being one of those of the shelved and safe, for all time, of whom I should have liked to begin by talking; one of those in whose favor discrimination has long since practically operated. She is in fact a signal instance of the way it does, with all its embarrassments, at last infallibly operate. A sharp short cut, one of the sharpest and shortest achieved, in this field, by the general judgment, came out, betimes, straight at her feet. Practically overlooked for thirty or forty years after her death, she perhaps really stands there for us as the prettiest possible example of that rectification of estimate, brought about by some slow clearance of stupidity, the half-century or so is capable of working round to. This tide has risen high on the opposite shore, the shore of appreciation — risen rather higher, I think, than the high-water mark, the highest, of her intrinsic merit and interest; though I grant indeed — as a point to be made — that we are dealing here in some degree with the tides so freely driven up, beyond their mere logical reach, by the stiff breeze of the commercial, in other words of the special bookselling spirit; an eager, active, interfering force which has a great many confusions of apparent value, a great many wild and wandering estimates, to answer for. For these distinctively mechanical and overdone reactions, of course, the critical spirit, even in its most relaxed mood, is not responsible. Responsible, rather, is the body of publishers, editors, illustrators, producers of the pleasant twaddle of magazines; who have found their "dear," our dear, everybody's dear, Jane so infinitely to their material purpose, so amenable to pretty reproduction in every variety of what is called tasteful, and in what seemingly proves to be saleable, form.

I do not, naturally, mean that she would be saleable if we had not more or less — beginning with Macaulay, her first slightly ponderous amoroso — lost our hearts to her; but I cannot help seeing her, a good deal, as in the same lucky box as the Brontés — lucky for the ultimate guerdon; a case of popularity (that in especial of the Yorkshire sisters), a beguiled infatuation, a sentimentalized vision, determined largely by the accidents and circumstances originally surrounding the manifestation of the genius — only with the reasons for the sentiment, in this latter connection, turned the other way. The key to Jane Austen's fortune with posterity has been in part the extraordinary grace of her facility, in fact of her unconsciousness: as if, at the most, for difficulty, for embarrassment, she sometimes, over her work-basket, her tapestry flowers, in the spare, cool drawing-room of other days, fell a-musing, lapsed too metaphorically, as one may say, into wool-gathering, and her dropped stitches, of these pardonable, of these precious moments, were afterwards picked up as little touches of human truth, little glimpses of steady vision, little master-strokes of imagination. The romantic tradition of the Brontés, with posterity, has been still more essentially helped, I think, by a force independent of any one of their applied faculties — by the attendant image of their dreary, their tragic history, their loneliness and poverty of life. That picture has been made to hang before us as insistently as the vividest page of "Jane Eyre" or of "Wuthering Heights." If these things were "stories," as we say, and stories of a lively interest, the medium from which they sprang was above all in itself a story, such a story as has fairly elbowed out the rights of appreciation, as has come at last to impose itself as an expression of the power concerned. The personal position of the three sisters, of the two in particular, had been marked, in short, with so sharp an accent that this accent has become for us the very tone of their united production. It covers and supplants their matter, their spirit, their style, their talent, their taste; it embodies, really, the most complete intellectual muddle, if the term be not extravagant, ever achieved, on a literary question, by our wonderful public. The question has scarce indeed been accepted as belonging to literature at all. Literature is an objective, a projected result; it is life that is the unconscious, the agitated, the struggling, floundering cause. But the fashion has been, in looking at the Brontés, so to confound the cause with the result that we cease to know, in the presence of such ecstasies, what we have hold of or what we are talking about. They represent, the ecstasies, the highwater mark of sentimental judgment.

These are but glimmering lanterns, however, you will say, to hang in the great dusky and deserted avenue that leads up to the seated statue of Balzac; and you are so far right, I am bound to admit, as that I place them there, no doubt, in a great measure, just to render the darkness visible. We do, collectively, with all our dimness of view, arrive at rough discriminations, and by one of the roughest of these the author of the "Comédie Humaine" has in a manner profited; we have for many a year taken his greatness for granted; but in the graceless and nerveless fashion of those who edge away from a classic or a bore. "Oh, yes, he is as 'great' as you like — so let us not talk of him!" My purpose has been to "talk" of him, and I find this form of greeting, therefore, and still more this form of parting, not at all adequate; failing as I do to point my moral unless I show that a really paying acquaintance with a writer can never take place if our recognition remains perfunctory. Our indolence and our ignorance may prefer the empty form; but the penalty and the humiliation come for us with the perception that when the consecration really takes place we have been excluded, so to speak, from the fun. I see no better proof that the great interesting art of which Balzac remains the greatest master is practically, round about us, a bankrupt and discredited art (discredited, of course I mean, for any directed and motived attention), than this very fact that we are so ready to beg off from knowing anything about him. Perfunctory rites, even, at present, are seldom rendered; and, amid the flood of verbiage for which the thousand new novels of the season find themselves a pretext in the newspapers, the name of the man who is really the father of us all, as we stand, is scarcely more mentioned than if he were not of the family.

I may at once intimate that the family strikes me as likely to recover its wasted heritage, and pull itself together for another chance, on condition only of shutting itself up, for an hour of wholesome heart-searching, with the image of its founder. He labors, I know, under the drawback of not being presentable as a classic — which is precisely why there would have seemed to be the less furtherance for regarding him as a bore. His situation in this respect is all his own: it was not given him to flower, for our convenience, into a single supreme felicity. His " successes " hang so together that analysis is almost baffled by his consistency, by his density. Even "Eugénie Grandet" is not a supreme felicity in the sense that this particular bloom is detachable from the cluster. The cluster is too thick, the stem too tough; before we know it, when we begin to pull, we have the whole branch about our heads — or it would indeed be more just to say we have the whole tree, if not the whole forest. It tells against a great worker, for free reference, that we must take his work in the mass; for, unfortunately, the circumstance that nothing of it surpassingly stands forth to represent the rest, to symbolize the whole, suggests a striking resemblance to work of other sorts. Of the mediocrities, and the bunglers too is it true that *they* do not supremely flower — as well as, further, of certain happy geniuses who have flowed in an uncontrolled, an undirected, above all in an unfiltered, current.

But the difference is that, for the most part, these loose and easy producers, the great resounding improvisatori, have not, in general, ended by imposing themselves; when we deal with them conclusively and, as I have said, for clearance of the slate, we deal with them by simplification, by elimination: which may very well be the revenge that time takes upon them to make up for the amount of space they happened immediately to occupy. They are still there, evidently; but they are there under this condition, which enters into account, at every instant, in any pious inquiry about them, and which is attached, intimately, to the appearance they finally wear for us, that the looseness and ease showing as their main sign in the time of their freshness is now a quality still more striking and often still more disconcerting. The weak sides in an artist are weakened with time, and the strong sides strengthened; so that it is never amiss, for duration, to have as many strong sides as possible. It is the only way we have yet made out — even in this age of superlative study of the cheap and easy — not to have so many weak ones as will eventually betray us. Balzac stands almost alone as an extemporizer achieving closeness and weight, and whom closeness and weight have preserved. My reason for speaking of him as an extemporizer I shall presently mention; but let me meanwhile frankly say that I speak of him, and can only speak, as a man of his own craft, an emulous fellow-worker, who has learned from him more of the lessons of the engaging mystery of fiction than from any one else, and who is conscious of so large a debt to repay that it has had positively to be discharged in instalments, as if one could never have at once all the required cash in hand.

When I am tempted, on occasion, to ask myself why we should, after all, so much as talk about the Novel, the wanton fable, against which, in so many ways, so showy an indictment may be drawn, I seem to see that the simplest plea is not to be sought in any attempted philosophy, in any abstract reason for our perversity or our levity. The real gloss upon these things is reflected from some great practitioner, some concrete instance of the art, some ample cloak under which we may gratefully crawl. It comes back, of course, to the example and the analogy of the Poet — with the abatement, however, that the Poet is most the Poet when he is preponderantly lyrical, when he speaks, laughing or crying, most directly from his individual heart, which throbs under the impressions of life. It is not the *image* of life that he thus expresses, so much as life itself, in its sources — so much as his own intimate, essential states and feelings. By the time he has begun to collect anecdotes, to tell stories, to represent scenes, to concern himself, that is, with the states and feelings of others, he is well on the way not to be the Poet pure and simple. The lyrical element, all the same, abides in him, and it is by this element that he is connected with what is most splendid in his expression. The lyrical instinct and tradition are immense in Shakespeare; which is why, great story-teller, great dramatist and painter, great lover, in short, of the image of life though he was, we need not press the case of his example. The lyrical element is not great, is in fact not present at all, in Balzac, in Scott (the Scott of the voluminous prose), nor in Thackeray, nor in Dickens — which is precisely why they are so essentially novelists, so almost exclusively lovers of the image of life. It *is* great, or it is at all events largely present, in such a writer as George Sand — which is doubtless why we take her for a novelist in a much looser sense than the others we have named. It is considerable in that bright particular genius of our own day, George Meredith, who so strikes us as hitching winged horses to the chariot of his prose

—steeds who prance and dance and caracole, who strain the traces, attempt to quit the ground, and yearn for the upper air. Balzac, with huge feet fairly ploughing the sand of our desert, is on the other hand the very type and model of the projector and creator; so that when I think, either with envy or with terror, of the nature and the effort of the Novelist, I think of something that reaches its highest expression in him. That is why those of us who, as fellow-craftsmen, have once caught a glimpse of this value in him, can never quite rest from hanging about him; that is why he seems to have all that the others have to tell us, with more, besides, that is all his own. He lived and breathed in his medium, and the fact that he was able to achieve in it, as man and as artist, so crowded a career, remains for us one of the most puzzling problems — I scarce know whether to say of literature or of life. He is himself a figure more extraor-

THE LESSON OF

dinary than any he drew, and the fascination may still be endless of all the questions he puts to us and of the answers for which we feel ourselves helpless.

He died, as we sufficiently remember, at fifty — worn out with work and thought and passion; the passion, I mean, that he had put into his mighty plan and that had ridden him like an infliction of the gods. He began, a friendless and penniless young provincial, to write early, and to write very badly, and it was not till well toward his thirtieth year, with the conception of the "Comédie Humaine," as we all again remember, that he found his right ground, found his feet and his voice. This huge distributed, divided and sub-divided picture of the life of France in his time, a picture bristling with imagination and information, with fancies and facts and figures, a world of special and general insight, a rank tropical forest of detail and specification, but with the strong breath of genius forever circulating through it and shaking the treetops to a mighty murmur, got itself hung before us in the space of twenty short years. The achievement remains one of the most inscrutable, one of the unfathomable, final facts in the history of art, and if, as I have said, the author himself has his own surpassing objectivity, it is just because of this challenge his figure constitutes for any other painter of life, inflamed with ingenuity, who should feel the temptation to represent or explain him. How represent, how explain him, as a concrete active energy? How depict him, we ask ourselves, *at* his huge conceived and accepted task, how reconcile such dissemination with such intensity, the collection and possession of so vast a number of facts with so rich a presentation of each? The elements of the world he set up before us, with all its insistent particulars, these elements were not, for him, a direct revelation — of so large a part of life is it true that

THE LESSON OF

we can know it only by living, and that living is the process that, in our mortal span, makes the largest demand on our time. How could a man have lived at large so much if, in the service of art, he had so much abstracted and condensed himself? How could he have so much abstracted and condensed himself if, in the service of life, he had felt and fought and acted, had labored and suffered, so much as a private in the ranks? The wealth and strength of his temperament indeed partly answer the question and partly obscure it. He could so extend his existence partly because he vibrated to so many kinds of contact and curiosity. To vibrate intellectually was his motive, but it magnified, all the while, it multiplied his experience. He could live at large, in short, because he was always living in the particular necessary, the particular intended connection — was always astride of his imagination, always charging, with his heavy, his heroic lance in rest, at every object that sprang up in his path. But as he was at the same time always fencing himself in against the personal adventure, the personal experience, in order to preserve himself for converting it into history, how did experience, in the immediate sense, still get itself saved? — or, to put it as simply as possible, where, with so strenuous a conception of the use of material, was material itself so strenuously quarried? Out of what mines, by what innumerable tortuous channels, in what endless winding procession of laden chariots and tugging teams and marching elephants, did the immense consignments required for his work reach him?

The point at which the emulous admirer, however diminished by comparison, may most closely approach him is, it seems to me, through the low portal of envy, so irresistibly do we lose ourselves in the vision of the quantity of life with which his imagination communicated. Quantity and intensity are at once and together his sign; the truth being that his energy did not press hard in some places only to press lightly in others, did not lay it on thick here or there to lay it on thin elsewhere, did not seek the appearance of extent and number by faintness of evocation, by shallow soundings, or by the mere sketchiness of suggestion that dispenses, for reference and verification, with the book, the total collection of human documents, with what we call "chapter and verse." He never throws dust in our eyes, save only the fine gold-dust through the haze of which his own romantic vision operates; never does it, I mean, when he is pretending not to do it, pretending to give us the full statement of his case, to deal with the facts of the spectacle surrounding him. Then he goes in, as we say, for a portentous clearness, a reproduction of the real on the scale of the real — with a definiteness actually proportionate; though a clearness that in truth sometimes fails (like the sight of the forest of the adage, which fails for the presence of the trees), through the positive monstrosity of his effort. He sees and presents too many facts — facts of history, of property, of genealogy, of topography, of sociology, and has too many ideas and images about them; their value is thus threatened with submersion by the flood of general reference in which they float, by their quantity of indicated relation to other facts, which break against them like waves of a high tide. He may thus at times become obscure from his very habit of striking too many matches; or we may at least say of him, out of our wondering loyalty, that the light he produces is, beyond that of any other corner of the great planted garden of romance, thick and rich and heavy — interesting, so to speak, on its own account.

There would be much to say, I think, had we only a little more time, on this question of the projected light of the individual strong temperament in fiction — the color of the air with which this, that or the other painter of life (as we call them all), more or less unconsciously suffuses his picture. I say unconsciously because I speak here of an effect of atmosphere largely, if not wholly, distinct from the effect sought on behalf of the special subject to be treated; something that proceeds from the contemplative mind itself, the very complexion of the mirror in which the material is reflected. This is of the nature of the man himself — an emanation of his spirit, temper, history; it springs from his very presence, his spiritual presence, in his work, and is, in so far, not a matter of calculation and artistry. All a matter of his own, in a word, for each seer of visions, the particular tone of the medium in which each vision, each clustered group of persons and places and objects, is bathed. Just how, accordingly, does the light of the world, the projected, painted, peopled, poetized, realized world, the furnished and fitted world into which we are beguiled for the holiday excursions, cheap trips or dear, of the eternally amusable, eternally dupeable voyaging mind — just how does this strike us as different in Fielding and in Richardson, in Scott and in Dumas, in Dickens and in Thackeray, in Hawthorne and in Meredith, in George Eliot and in George Sand, in Jane Austen and in Charlotte Bronté? Do we not feel the general landscape evoked by each of the more or less magical wands to which I have given name, not to open itself under the same sun that hangs over the neighboring scene, not to receive the solar rays at the same angle, not to exhibit its shadows with the same intensity or the same sharpness; not, in short, to seem to belong to the same time of day or same state of the weather? Why is it that the life that overflows in Dickens seems to me always to go on in the morning, or in the very earliest hours of the afternoon at most, and in a vast apartment that appears to have windows, large, uncurtained and rather unwashed windows, on all sides at once? Why is it that in George Eliot the sun sinks forever to the west, and the shadows are long, and the afternoon wanes, and the trees vaguely rustle, and the color of the day is much inclined to yellow? Why is it that in Charlotte Brontë we move through an endless autumn? Why is it that in Jane Austen we sit quite resigned in an arrested spring? Why does Hawthorne give us the afternoon hour later than any one else? — oh, late, late, quite uncannily late, and as if it were always winter outside? But I am wasting the very minutes I pretended, at the start, to cherish, and am only sustained through my levity by seeing you watch for the time of day or season of the year or state of the weather that I shall fasten upon the complicated clock-face of Thackeray. I do, I think, see his light also — see it very much as the light (a different thing from the mere dull dusk) of rainy days in " residential" streets ; but we are not, after all, talking of him, and, though Balzac's waiting power has proved itself, this half-century, immense, I must not too much presume upon it.

The question of the color of Balzac's air and the time of *his* day would indeed here easily solicit our ingenuity — were I at liberty to say more than one thing about it. It is rich and thick, the mixture of sun and shade diffused through the " Comédie Humaine" — a mixture richer and thicker, and representing an absolutely greater quantity of " atmosphere," than we shall find prevailing within the compass of any other suspended frame. That is how we see him, living in his garden, and it is by reason of the (restless energy) with which he circulated there that I hold his fortune and his privilege, in spite of the burden of

THE LESSON OF

his toil and the brevity of his immediate reward, to have been before any others enviable. It is strange enough, but what most abides with us, as we follow his steps, is a sense of the intellectual luxury he enjoyed. To focus him at all, for a single occasion, we have to simplify, and this wealth of his vicarious experience forms the side, moreover, on which he is most attaching for those who take an interest in the real play of the imagination. From the moment our imagination plays at all, of course, and from the moment we try to catch and preserve the pictures it throws off, from that moment we too, in our comparatively feeble way, live vicariously — succeed in opening a series of dusky passages in which, with a more or less childlike ingenuity, we can romp to and fro. Our passages are mainly short and dark, however; we soon come to the end of them — dead walls, without resonance, in presence of which the candle goes out and the game stops, and we have only to retrace our steps. Balzac's luxury, as I call it, was in the extraordinary number and length of his radiating and ramifying corridors — the labyrinth in which he finally lost himself. What it comes back to, in other words, is the intensity with which we live — and his intensity is recorded for us on every page of his work.

It is a question, you see, of *penetrating* into a subject; his corridors always went further and further and further; which is but another way of expressing his inordinate passion for detail. It matters nothing — nothing for my present contention — that this extravagance is also his great fault; in spite, too, of its all being detail vivified and related, characteristic and constructive, essentially prescribed by the terms of his plan. The relations of parts to each other are at moments multiplied almost to madness — which is at the same time just why they give us the measure of his hallucination, make up the greatness of his intellectual adventure. His plan was to handle, primarily, not a world of ideas, animated by figures representing these ideas; but the packed and constituted, the palpable, proveable world before him, by the study of which ideas would inevitably find themselves thrown up. If the happy fate is accordingly to *partake* of life, actively, assertively, not passively, narrowly, in mere sensibility and sufferance, the happiness has been greatest when the faculty employed has been largest. We employ different faculties — some of us only our arms and our legs and our stomach; Balzac employed most what he possessed in largest quantity. This is where his work ceases in a manner to mystify us — this is where we make out how he did quarry his material: it is the sole solution to an otherwise baffling problem. He collected his experience within himself: no other economy explains his achievement;

this thrift alone, remarkable yet thinkable, embodies the necessary miracle. His system of cellular confinement, in the interest of the miracle, was positively that of a Benedictine monk leading his life within the four walls of his convent and bent, the year round, over the smooth parchment on which, with wondrous illumination and enhancement of gold and crimson and blue, he inscribes the glories of the faith and the legends of the saints. Balzac's view of himself was indeed in a manner the monkish one; he was most at ease, while he wrought, in the white gown and cowl — an image of him that the friendly art of his time has handed down to us. Only, as happened, his subject of illumination was the legends not merely of the saints, but of the much more numerous uncanonized strugglers and sinners, an acquaintance with whose attributes was not all to be gathered in the place of piety itself; not even from the faintest ink of old records, the mild lips of old brothers, or the painted glass of church windows.

This is where envy does follow him, for to have so many other human cases, so many other personal predicaments to get into, up to one's chin, is verily to be able to get out of one's own box. And it was up to his chin, constantly, that he sank in his illusion — not, as the weak and timid in this line do, only up to his ankles or his knees. The figures he sees begin immediately to bristle with all their characteristics. Every mark and sign, outward and inward, that they possess; every virtue and every vice, every strength and every weakness, every passion and every habit, the sound of their voices, the expression of their eyes, the tricks of feature and limb, the buttons on their clothes, the food on their plates, the money in their pockets, the furniture in their houses, the secrets in their breasts, are all things that interest, that concern, that command him, and that have, for the picture, significance, relation and value. It is a prodigious multiplication of values, and thereby a prodigious entertainment of the vision — on the condition the vision can bear it. Bearing it — that is *our* bearing it — is a serious matter; for the appeal is truly to that faculty of attention out of which we are educating ourselves as hard as we possibly can; educating ourselves with such complacency, with such boisterous high spirits, that we may already be said to have practically lost it — with the consequence that any work of art or of criticism making a demand on it is by that fact essentially discredited. It takes attention not only to thread the labyrinth of the " Comédie Humaine," but to keep our author himself in view, in the relations in which we thus image him. But if we can muster it, as I say, in sufficient quantity, we thus walk with him in the great glazed gallery of his thought;

the long, lighted and pictured ambulatory where the endless series of windows, on one side, hangs over his revolutionized, ravaged, yet partly restored and reinstated garden of France, and where, on the other, the figures and the portraits we fancy stepping down to meet him climb back into their frames, larger and smaller, and take up position and expression as he desired they shall look out and compose.

We have lately had a literary case of the same general family as the case of Balzac, and in presence of which some of the same speculations come up: I had occasion, not long since, after the death of Émile Zola, to attempt an appreciation of *his* extraordinary performance — his series of the " Rougon-Macquart " constituting in fact, in the library of the fiction that can hope in some degree to live, a monument to the idea of plenitude, of comprehension and variety, second only to the

"Comédie Humaine." The question presented itself, in respect to Zola's ability and Zola's career, with a different proportion and value, I quite recognize, and wearing a much less distinguished face; but it was there to be met, none the less, on the very threshold, and all the more because this was just where he himself had placed it. His idea had been, from the first, in a word, to lose no time — as if one could have experience, even the mere amount requisite for showing others as having it, *without* losing time! — and yet the degree in which he too, so handicapped, has achieved valid expression is such as still to stagger us. He had had inordinately to simplify — had had to leave out the life of the soul, practically, and confine himself to the life of the instincts, of the more immediate passions, such as can be easily and promptly caught in the fact. He had had, in a word, to confine himself almost entirely to the impulses and agitations that men and women are possessed by in common, and to take them as exhibited in mass and number, so that, being writ larger, they might likewise be more easily read. He met and solved, in this manner, his difficulty — the difficulty of knowing, and of showing, of life, only what his "notes" would account for. But it is in the *waste*, I think, much rather — the waste of time, of passion, of curiosity, of contact — that true initiation resides; so that the most wonderful adventures of the artist's spirit are those, immensely quickening for his "authority," that are yet not reducible to his notes. It is exactly here that we get the difference between such a solid, square, symmetrical structure as "Les Rougon-Macquart," vitiated, in a high degree, by its mechanical side, and the monument left by Balzac — without the example of which, I surmise, Zola's work would not have existed. The mystic process of the crucible, the transformation of the material under æsthetic heat, is, in the "Comédie Humaine," thanks to an intenser and more submissive fusion, completer, and also finer; for if the commoner and more wayside passions and conditions are, in the various episodes there, at no time gathered into so large and so thick an illustrative bunch, yet on the other hand they are shown much more freely at play in the individual case — and the individual case it is that permits of supreme fineness. It is hard to say where Zola is fine; whereas it is often, for pages together, hard to say where Balzac is, even under the weight of his too ponderous personality, not. The most fundamental and general sign of the novel, from one desperate experiment to another, is its being everywhere an effort at *representation* — this is the beginning and the end of it: wherefore it was that one could say at last, with account taken of everything, that Zola's performance, on his immense scale, was an extraordinary show of representation imitated. The imitation in places — notably and admirably, for instance, in "L'Assommoir" — breaks through into something that we take for reality; but, for the most part, the separating rift, the determining difference, holds its course straight, prevents the attempted process from becoming the sound, straight, whole thing that is given us by those who have really *bought* their information. This is where Balzac remains unshaken — in our feeling that, with all his faults of pedantry, ponderosity, pretentiousness, bad taste and charmless form, his spirit has somehow paid for its knowledge. His subject is again and again the complicated human creature or human condition; and it is with these complications as if he knew them, as Shakespeare knew them, by his charged consciousness, by the history of his soul and the direct exposure of his sensibility. This source of supply he found, forever — and one may indeed say he mostly left — sitting at his fireside; where it constituted the company with which I see him shut up and his practical intimacy with which, during such orgies and debauches of intellectual passion, might earn itself that name of high personal good fortune that I have applied.

Let me say, definitely, that I hold several of his faults to be grave, and that if there were any question of time for it I should like to speak of them; but let me add, as promptly, that they are faults, on the whole, of execution, flaws in the casting, accidents of the process: they never come back to that fault in the artist, in the novelist, that amounts most completely to a failure of dignity, the absence of saturation with his idea. When saturation fails no other presence really avails; as when, on the other hand, it operates, no failure of method fatally interferes. There is never in Balzac that damning interfer-

THE LESSON OF

ence which consists of the painter's not seeing, not possessing, his image; not having fixed his creature and his creature's conditions. "Balzac aime sa Valérie," says Taine, in his great essay — so much the finest thing ever written on our author — speaking of the way in which the awful little Madame Marneffe of "Les Parents Pauvres" is drawn, and of the long rope, for her acting herself out, that her creator's participation in her reality assures her. He has been contrasting her, as it happens, with Thackeray's Becky Sharp or rather with Thackeray's attitude toward Becky, and the marked jealousy of her freedom that Thackeray exhibits from the first. I remember reading at the time of the publication of Taine's study — though it was long, long ago — a phrase in an English review of the volume which seemed to my limited perception, even in extreme youth, to deserve the highest prize ever bestowed on critical stupidity undisguised.

If Balzac loved his Valérie, said this commentator, that only showed Balzac's extraordinary taste; the truth being really, throughout, that it was just through this love of each seized identity, and of the sharpest and liveliest identities most, that Madame Marneffe's creator was able to marshal his array at all. The love, as we call it, the joy in their communicated and exhibited movement, in their standing on their feet and going of themselves and acting out their characters, was what rendered possible the saturation I speak of; what supplied him, through the inevitable gaps of his preparation and the crevices of his prison, his long prison of labor, a short cut to the knowledge he required. It was by loving them — as the terms of his subject and the nuggets of his mine — that he knew them; it was not by knowing them that he loved.

He at all events robustly loved the sense of another explored, assumed, assimilated identity — enjoyed it as the hand enjoys the glove when the glove ideally fits. My image indeed is loose; for what he liked was absolutely to get into the constituted consciousness, into all the clothes, gloves and whatever else, into the very skin and bones, of the habited, featured, colored, articulated form of life that he desired to present. How do we know given persons, for any purpose of demonstration, unless we know their situation for themselves, unless we see it from their point of vision, that is from their point of pressing consciousness or sensation?— without our allowing for which there is no appreciation. Balzac loved his Valérie then as Thackeray did not love his Becky, or his Blanche Amory in "Pendennis." But his prompting was not to expose her; it could only be, on the contrary — intensely aware as he was of all the lengths she might go, and paternally, maternally alarmed about them — to cover her up and protect her, in the interest of her special genius and freedom. All his impulse was to *la faire valoir*, to give her all her value, just as Thackeray's attitude was the opposite one, a desire positively to expose and desecrate poor Becky — to follow her up, catch her in the act and bring her to shame: though with a mitigation, an admiration, an inconsequence, now and then wrested from him by an instinct finer, in his mind, than the so-called "moral" eagerness. The English writer wants to make sure, first of all, of your moral judgment; the French is willing, while it waits a little, to risk, for the sake of his subject and its interest, your spiritual salvation. Madame Marneffe, detrimental, fatal as she is, is "exposed," so far as anything in life, or in art, may be, by the working-out of the situation and the subject themselves; so that when they have done what they would, what they logically had to, with her, we are ready to take it from them.

THE LESSON OF

We do not feel, very irritatedly, very lecturedly, in other words with superfluous edification, that she has been sacrificed. Who can say, on the contrary, that Blanche Amory, in "Pendennis," with the author's lash about her little bare white back from the first — who can feel that she has *not* been sacrificed, or that her little bareness and whiteness, and all the rest of her, have been, by such a process, presented as they had a right to demand?

It all comes back, in fine, to that respect for the liberty of the subject which I should be willing to name as *the* great sign of the painter of the first order. Such a witness to the human comedy fairly holds his breath for fear of arresting or diverting that natural license; the witness who begins to breathe so uneasily in presence of it that his respiration not only warns off the little prowling or playing creature he is supposed to be studying, but drowns, for our ears, the ingenuous sounds of the animal, as well as the general, truthful hum of the human scene at large — this demonstrator has no sufficient warrant for his task. And if such an induction as this is largely the moral of our renewed glance at Balzac, there is a lesson, of a more essential sort, I think, folded still deeper within — the lesson that there is no convincing art that is not ruinously expensive. I am unwilling to say, in the presence of such of his successors as George Eliot and Tolstoi and Zola (to name, for convenience, only three of them), that he was the last of the novelists to do the thing handsomely; but I will say that we get the impression at least of his having had more to spend. Many of those who have followed him affect us as doing it, in the vulgar phrase, " on the cheap; " by reason mainly, no doubt, of their having been, all helplessly, foredoomed to cheapness. Nothing counts, of course, in art, but the excellent; nothing exists, however briefly, for estimation, for appre-

THE LESSON OF

ciation, but the superlative — always in its kind; and who shall declare that the severe economy of the vast majority of those apparently emulous of the attempt to "render" the human subject and the human scene proceeds from anything worse than the consciousness of a limited capital? This flourishing frugality operates happily, no doubt — given all the circumstances — for the novelist; but it has had terrible results for the novel, so far as the novel is a form with which criticism may be moved to concern itself. Its misfortune, its discredit, what I have called its bankrupt state among us, is the not unnatural consequence of its having ceased, for the most part, to be artistically interesting. It has become an object of easy manufacture, showing on every side the stamp of the machine; it has become the article of commerce, produced in quantity, and as we so see it we inevitably turn from it, under the rare visitations of the critical impulse, to compare it with those more precious products of the same general nature that we used to think of as belonging to the class of the hand-made.

The lesson of Balzac, under this comparison, is extremely various, and I should prepare myself much too large a task were I to attempt a list of the separate truths he brings home. I have to choose among them, and I choose the most important; the three or four that more or less include the others. In reading him over, in opening him almost anywhere to-day, what immediately strikes us is the part assigned by him, in any picture, to the *conditions* of the creatures with whom he is concerned. Contrasted with him other prose painters of life scarce seem to see the conditions at all. He clearly held pretended portrayal as nothing, as less than nothing, as a most vain thing, unless it should be, in spirit and intention, the art of complete representation. "Complete" is of course a great word, and there is no art at all, we are often reminded, that is not on too many sides an abject compromise. The element of compromise is always there; it is of the essence; we live with it, and it may serve to keep us humble. The formula of the whole matter is sufficiently expressed perhaps in a reply I found myself once making to an inspired but discouraged friend, a fellow-craftsman who had declared in his despair that there was no use trying, that it was a form, the novel, absolutely too difficult. "Too difficult indeed; yet there is one way to master it — which is to pretend consistently that it is n't." We are all of us, all the while, pretending — as consistently as we can — that it is n't, and Balzac's great glory is that he pretended hardest. He never had to pretend so hard as when he addressed himself to that evocation of the medium, that distillation of the natural and social air, of which I speak, the things that most require on the part of the painter preliminary possession — so definitely require it that, terrified at the requisition when conscious of it, many a painter prefers to beg the whole question. He has thus, this ingenious person, to invent some *other* way of making his characters interesting — some other way, that is, than the arduous way, demanding so much consideration, of presenting them to us. They are interesting, in fact, as subjects of fate, the figures round whom a situation closes, in proportion as, sharing their existence, we feel where fate comes in and just how it gets at them. In the void they are not interesting — and Balzac, like Nature herself, abhorred a vacuum. Their situation takes hold of us because it is theirs, not because it is somebody's, any one's, that of creatures unidentified. Therefore it is not superfluous that their identity shall first be established for us, and their adventures, in that measure, have a relation to it, and therewith an appreciability. There is no such thing in the world as an adventure pure and simple; there is only mine and yours, and his and hers — it being the greatest adventure of all, I verily think, just to *be* you or I, just to be he or she. To Balzac's imagination that was indeed in itself an immense adventure — and nothing appealed to him more than to show *how* we all are, and how we are placed and built-in for being so. What befalls us is but another name for the way our circumstances press upon us — so that an account of what befalls us is an account of our circumstances.

Add to this, then, that the fusion of all the elements of the picture, under his hand, is complete — of what people are with what they do, of what they do with what they are, of the action with the agents, of the medium with the action, of all the parts of the drama with each other. Such a production as " Le Père Goriot " for example, or as "Eugénie Grandet," or as "Le Curé de Village," has, in respect to this fusion, a kind of inscrutable perfection. The situation sits shrouded in its circumstances, and then, by its inner expansive force, emerges from them, the action marches, to the rich rustle of this great tragic and ironic train, the embroidered heroic mantle, with an art of keeping together that makes of "Le Père Goriot" in especial a supreme case of composition, a model of that high virtue that we know as economy of effect, economy of line and touch. An inveterate sense of proportion was not, in general, Balzac's distinguishing mark; but with great talents one has great surprises, and the effect of this large handling of the conditions was more often than not to make the work, whatever it might be, appear admirably composed. Of all the costly charms of a "story" this interest derived from composition is the costliest — and there is perhaps no better proof of our present penury than the fact that, in general, when one makes a plea for it, the plea might seemingly (for all it is understood!) be for trigonometry or osteology. "Composition?—what may that happen to *be*, and, whatever it is, what has it to do with the matter?" I shall take for granted here that every one perfectly knows, for without that assumption I shall not be able to wind up, as I must immediately do. The presence of the conditions, when really presented, when made vivid, provides for the action —which is, from step to step, constantly implied in them; whereas the process of suspending the action in the void and dressing it there with the tinkling bells of what is called dialogue only makes no provision at all for the other interest. There are two elements of the art of the novelist which, as they present, I think, the greatest difficulty, tend thereby most to fascinate us: in the first place that mystery of the foreshortened procession of facts and figures, of appearances of whatever sort, which is in some lights but another name for the picture governed by the principle of composition, and which has at any rate as little as possible in common with the method now usual among us, the juxtaposition of items emulating the column of numbers of a schoolboy's sum in addition. It is the art of the brush, I know, as opposed to the art of the slate-pencil; but to the art of the brush the novel must return, I hold, to recover whatever may be still recoverable of its sacrificed honor.

The second difficulty that I commend for its fascination, at all events, the most attaching when met and the most rewarding when triumphantly met — though I hasten to add that it also strikes me as not only the least "met," in general, but the least suspected — this second difficulty is that of representing, to put it simply, the lapse of time, the duration of the subject: representing it, that is, more subtly than by a blank space, or a row of stars, on the historic page. With the blank space and the row of stars Balzac's genius had no affinity, and he is therefore as unlike as possible those narrators — so numerous, all round us, it would appear, to-day in especial — the succession of whose steps and stages, the development of whose action, in the given case, affects us as occupying but a week or two. No one begins, to my sense, to handle the time-element and produce the time-effect with the authority of Balzac in his amplest sweeps — by which I am far from meaning in his longest passages. That study of the foreshortened image, of the neglect of which I suggest the ill consequence, is precisely the enemy of the tiresome procession of would-be narrative items, seen all in profile, like the rail-heads of a fence; a substitute for the baser device of accounting for the time-quantity by mere quantity of statement. Quality and manner of statement account for it in a finer way — always assuming, as I say, that unless it is accounted for nothing else really is. The fashion of our day is to account for it almost exclusively by an inordinate abuse of the colloquial resource, of the report, from page to page, from chapter to chapter, from beginning to end, of the talk, between the persons involved, in which situation and action may be conceived as registered. Talk between persons is perhaps, of all the parts of the novelist's plan, the part that Balzac most scrupulously weighed and measured and kept in its place; judging it, I think — though he perhaps even had an undue suspicion of its possible cheapness, as feeling it the thing that can least afford to be cheap — a precious and supreme resource, the very flower of illustration of the subject and thereby not to be inconsiderately discounted. It was his view, discernibly, that the flower must keep its bloom, or in other words not be too much handled, in order to have a fragrance when nothing but its fragrance will serve.

It was his view indeed positively that there is a *law* in these things, and that, admirable for illustration, functional for illustration, dialogue has its function perverted, and therewith its life destroyed, when forced, all clumsily, into the constructive office. It is in the drama, of course, that it is constructive; but the drama lives by a law so different, verily, that everything that is right for it seems wrong for the prose picture, and everything that is right for the prose picture addressed directly, in turn, to the betrayal of the "play." These are questions, however, that bore deep — if I have successfully braved the danger that they absolutely do bore; so that I must content myself, as a glance at this point, with the claim for the author of "Le Père Goriot" that colloquial illustration, in his work, suffers less, on the whole, than in any other I know, from its attendant, its besetting and haunting penalty of springing, unless watched, a leak in its effect. It is as if the master of the ship were keeping his eye on the pump; the pump, I mean, of relief and alternation, the pump that keeps the vessel free of too much water. We must always remember that, save in the cases where "dialogue" is organic, is the very law of the game — in which case, as I say, the game is another business altogether — it is essentially the fluid element: as, for instance (to cite, conveniently, Balzac's most eminent prose contemporary), was strikingly its character in the elder Dumas; just as its character in the younger, the dramatist, illustrates supremely what I call the other game. The current, in old Dumas, the large, loose, facile flood of talked movement, talked interest, as much as you will, is, in virtue of this fluidity, a current indeed, with so little of wrought texture that we float and splash in it; feeling it thus resemble much more some capacious tepid tank than the figured tapestry, all overscored with objects in fine perspective, which symbolizes to me (if one may have a symbol) the last word of the achieved fable. Such a tapestry, with its wealth of expression of its subject, with its myriad ordered stitches, its harmonies of tone and felicities of taste, is a work, above all, of closeness — and therefore the more pertinent image here as it is in the name of closeness that I am inviting you to let Balzac once more appeal to you.

It will strike you perhaps that I speak as if we all, as if you all, without exception were novelists, haunting the back shop, the laboratory, or, more nobly expressed, the inner shrine of the temple; but such assumptions, in this age of print — if I may not say this age of poetry — are perhaps never too wide of the mark, and I have at any rate taken your interest sufficiently for granted to ask you to close up with me for an hour at the feet of the master of us all. Many of us may stray, but he always remains — he is fixed by virtue of his weight. Do not look too knowing at that — as a hint that you were already conscious he is heavy, and that if this is what I have mainly to suggest my lesson might have been spared. He is, I grant, too heavy to be moved; many of us may stray and straggle, as I say — since we have not his inaptitude largely to circulate. There is none the less such an odd condition as circulating without motion, and I am not so sure that even in our own way we do move. We do not, at any rate, get away from him; he is behind us, at the worst, when he is not before, and I feel that any course about the country we explore is ever best held by keeping him, through the trees of the forest, in sight. So far as we do move, we move round him;

every road comes back to him; he sits there, in spite of us, so massively, for orientation. "Heavy" therefore if we like, but heavy because weighted with his fortune; the extraordinary fortune that has survived all the extravagance of his career, his twenty years of royal intellectual spending, and that has done so by reason of the rare value of the original property — the high, prime genius so tied-up from him that that was safe. And "that," through all that has come and gone, has steadily, has enormously appreciated. Let us then also, if we see him, in the sacred grove, as our towering idol, see him as gilded thick, with so much gold — plated and burnished and bright, in the manner of towering idols. It is for the lighter and looser and poorer among us to be gilded thin!

The Riverside Press
Electrotyped and printed by H. O. Houghton & Co.
Cambridge, Mass., U. S. A.

"Art deals with what we see... but it has no sooner done this than it has to take account of a process"

"hunt" for Lambert Strether; cytogenic paradigm...